Stage 1+
Songbirds Phonics

Teaching Notes

Clare Kirtley

Cont

C000046844

Introduction

These books present highly decodable texts that children can read by sounding out and blending. They provide a reading context through which children can discover and understand that there is a code to reading. The explicit usefulness of phonics is emphasized in a variety of exciting reading books, all by popular, award winning children's author Julia Donaldson.

The focus phonics are listed on the cover of each book. By introducing these and the skills of sounding out and blending prior to reading, the children will be equipped with the necessary knowledge to confidently and successfully read unfamiliar words in the books. The books consolidate letter-sound knowledge and practise the skills of sounding out and blending, reinforcing decoding as a reading strategy that children can use to become fluent, independent and capable readers. These notes describe activities to learn the focus phonics prior, during and after group or independent reading. The amount of time spent introducing the phonics prior to reading will of course depend on the ability of the children.

The inclusion of words that do not use the focus phonics being introduced or studied previously has been kept to a minimum while keeping the texts meaningful. Such words, often high frequency words, can be introduced and compared with the decodable words before studying the texts. The children can be encouraged to read such words in the text using several reading strategies such as sounding out, rereading to check it makes sense, context and sight vocabulary. Therefore such words are listed as 'Context' words.

These books provide the ideal resource for children to decode, understand and reflect on what has been written, responding to the varied ideas, themes and events and thus engaging in reading for pleasure. They fully support a synthetic approach to teaching reading and follow the introduction of grapheme-phoneme correspondences outlined in *Playing with Sounds*.

Glossary

Phoneme – a sound in a word (e.g. *cat, shop, sky, light* and *rain* all have three phonemes or three separate sounds)

Grapheme – a letter or sequence of letters that represents a phoneme (e.g in *rain* each of the three phonemes is represented by a grapheme *r – ai – n*; in *light* each of the three phonemes is represented by a grapheme, namely *l – igh – t*.

Context words – words which do not use the focus phonics but which are needed for the story.

Top Cat

Focus phonics
The sound made by: m c t p a o

Skills, concepts and knowledge covered by the Teaching Notes
Skills – Blend two or three sounds together to make words; Segment simple CVC words into their individual sounds

Concepts – Words consist of sounds; Sounds in words are represented by letters

Knowledge – Focus phonics

Example phonic words
am top cat pop

Context words
I

NLS Objectives	Early Learning Goals	Playing with Sounds	PiPs	Scotland	Wales	N Ireland
YR – W1, W2, W4, W14, S3, T1, T14 Y1 – W4, W5, W6	CLL 9, CLL 10	Phoneme-grapheme correspondences from Group 1 Card 9	Steps 2–4	Level A	Range: 1–6 Skills: 1, 2	Activities: a, b, c, e, f, h Outcomes: b, c, d, e, e, f, k

Sam's Pot

Focus phonics
The sound made by: s m c t g p a o

Skills, concepts and knowledge covered by the Teaching Notes
Skills – Blend three sounds together to make words; Segment simple CVC words into their individual sounds

Concepts – Words consist of sounds; Sounds in words are represented by letters

Knowledge – Focus phonics

Example phonic words
Tom got pot Pam Sam pat tap mop

Context words
a

NLS Objectives	Early Learning Goals	Playing with Sounds	PiPs	Scotland	Wales	N Ireland
YR – W1, W2, W4, W14, S3, S4, T1, T14 Y1 – W4, W5, W6	CLL 9, CLL 10	Phoneme-grapheme correspondences from Group 1 and 2 Card 9	Steps 2–4	Level A	Range: 1–6 Skills: 1, 2	Activities: a, b, c, e, f, h Outcomes: b, c, d, e, f, k

Bob Bug

Focus phonics
The sound made by:
r l d b f h i u s
m c t g p a o

Skills, concepts and knowledge covered by the Teaching Notes
Skills – Blend three sounds together to make words;
Segment simple CVC words into their individual sounds

Concepts – Words consist of sounds;
Sounds in words are represented by letters

Knowledge – Focus phonics

Example phonic words
Bob bug has mum His is big dad fit cup It lid cot rug bad rat hug

Context words
a

NLS Objectives	**Scotland**	**Wales**	**N Ireland**
YR – W2, W4, W14, T1, T15 Y1T1 – W4, W5, W6	Level A	Range: 1–6 Skills: 1, 2	Activities: a, b, c, e, f, h Outcomes: b, c, d, e, f, k

Early Learning Goals
CLL 9, CLL 10

Playing with Sounds
Phoneme-grapheme correspondences from Group 1 and 2 Card 10

PiPs
Steps 2–4

Dig, Dig, Dig!

Focus phonics
The sound made by:
r l d b f h i u
s m t g p a o
n

Skills, concepts and knowledge covered by the Teaching Notes
Skills – Blend three or four sounds together to make words;
Segment simple CVC words into their individual sounds

Concepts – Words consist of sounds;
Sounds in words are represented by letters

Knowledge – Focus phonics

Example phonic words
dig Tim his dog had fun dug up lot mud rag bus lid big tin in it lots bugs and

Context words
a of

NLS Objectives	**Scotland**	**Wales**	**N Ireland**
YR – W2, T1, T7, T15 Y1T1 – W4, W5, W6	Level A	Range: 1–6 Skills: 1, 2	Activities: a, b, c, e, f, h Outcomes: b, c, d, e, f, k

Early Learning Goals
CLL 9, CLL 10

Playing with Sounds
Phoneme-grapheme correspondences from Group 1 and 2 Card 10

PiPs
Steps 2–4

Zak and the Vet

Focus phonics
The sound made by:
v w y z j n k e
r d b f h i u
s m c t g a o

Skills, concepts and knowledge covered by the Teaching Notes
Skills – Blend three sounds together to make words; Segment simple CVC words into their individual sounds

Concepts – Words consist of sounds; Sounds in words are represented by letters; There can be more than one way to represent a sound

Knowledge – Focus phonics

Example phonic words
sit Zak did not ran in fog red van hit him Jen vet had bad cut get jab yes wag and went

Context words
a better He the to will

NLS Objectives	Scotland	Wales	N Ireland
YR – W2, W4, W14, T15 Y1T1 – W4, W5, W6	Level A	Range: 1–6 Skills: 1, 2	Activities: a, b, c, e, f, h Outcomes: b, c, d, e, f, k

Early Learning Goals
CLL 9, CLL 10

Playing with Sounds
Phoneme-grapheme correspondences from Group 1, 2 and 3 Card 11

PiPs
Steps 2–4

Mum Bug's Bag

Focus phonics
The sound made by:
w y z j n k e
r d b f h i u
s m c t g p a o

Skills, concepts and knowledge covered by the Teaching Notes
Skills – Blend three sounds together to make words; Segment simple CVC words into their individual sounds

Concepts – Words consist of sounds; Sounds in words are represented by letters; There can be more than one way to represent a sound

Knowledge – Focus phonics

Example phonic words
Mum Bug has red bag zip can fit pen in fan bun pot jam get wet yuk big gets and

Context words
a her hole of the

NLS Objectives	Scotland	Wales	N Ireland
YR – W2, W4, T1, T14 Y1T1 – W4, W5, W6	Level A	Range: 1–6 Skills: 1, 2	Activities: a, b, c, e, f, h Outcomes: b, c, d, e, f, k

Early Learning Goals
CLL 9, CLL 10

Playing with Sounds
Phoneme-grapheme correspondences from Group 1, 2 and 3 Card 11

PiPs
Steps 2–4

Top Cat

Focus phonics			
m	am mat	*p*	top pop
c	cat	*a*	am cat mat
t	top cat mat	*o*	top pop

Introducing the phonics

- Make a display of objects which begin with each of the focus sounds (e.g. *mat, cup, teddy, pan, ant, orange*). Encourage children to draw pictures of objects or make models out of construction, to add to the display. Give the children different pens, pencils and chalks to practise writing the letters.
- Make letter cards by writing the focus letters on individual pieces of card. Stress the correct letter formation as you do so and encourage the children to skywrite the letters.
- *Quick Sounds*
  Ask the children to say the sound usually made by each letter as you point to it. Vary the order.
- *Blending Sounds*
  Draw three boxes in a row, as a phoneme frame, on a whiteboard. Display the letter cards (or magnetic letters) around it. Pick three cards and place them, one in each box, to make a word (*cat, mat, pat, top, pop, mop, cop, cot, pot*). Tell the children that each of these letters makes one sound in a word. Ask the children to say the sound of each letter as you point to it. Then tell the children that you are going to blend the letters together to make the word. Say the sounds altogether and ask the children to say them with you to read the word.

Before reading

- Ask the children to find the title. Explain that the *top* person can mean the most important person in a group and that the *top* of something is also the highest part of something. For example, the *top* of a mountain is the highest point.
- Ask the children to look at the letters in the box on the back cover of their books and tell you the sound usually made by each letter in words. Can the children think of any words that begin with each of these letters? (They can look at your display if you have one.)
- Tell the children that most of the words in this book use these letters so they can sound out each letter and blend them together to read the words just as you did together when reading the words you wrote in the phoneme frame.
- Ask the children to find and point to the first word on the first page.

During reading

- Read the first word *I* and explain that this is a word they will meet a lot in stories and the children should look out for it in this story.
- Ask the children to point at the text, moving along the line from left to right.
- Encourage each of the children to read the whole book at his or her own pace, pointing at the words, sounding out and blending words they do not recognise and remembering to look out for the word *I*. Listen in to each child reading and provide lots of praise and support if necessary.
- Praise them if they can match one spoken word to one written word.
- Praise the children for sounding out and blending sounds to read words.

Assessment

Observe the children to check that they can:
- point at the text, moving along the line from left to right
- confidently give the sound for all the focus letters
- successfully blend the two sounds for *am* together and recognise it as the word *am*
- successfully blend the three sounds for *top* together and recognise it as the word *top*
- recognise repeated words
- notice the change in word order on pages 2 and 4.

Emphasise and model these skills for any child who needs help.

Returning to the text

Ask the children to

- Find a word in the text beginning with the sound c, sound out all the letters in the word and then blend them together to read the word. Repeat for a then t.
- Find the picture of the cat sat on the mat. Think of other words which rhyme with cat (e.g. chat, bat, hat, pat, rat).
- Shut the book and segment cat into its separate sounds ready for writing. Have a go at writing cat on a whiteboard. Blend the sounds together again. Find it in the book to check.
- Change One Letter
  Change one letter of cat to write pat, then mat, then map.

Assessment

Observe the children to check that they can:

- remember the letter that makes the sound c, the sound a and the sound t
- generate words which rhyme with cat.

Model the appropriate responses for children who need help. Follow this up with further practice using the Blending Activity, Letter Pattern Activity and Segmenting Activity for Top Cat on the Songbirds CD-ROM, as well as additional practice reading Top Cat using the Talking Story version.

Where next?

Further practice

- Ask the children to write top on a whiteboard. Think of other words that rhyme with top (mop, cop) and segment the new words into their separate sounds, saying each sound in isolation as you write it. Then blend the sounds together while pointing at each sound.

Extension

Ask the children to write and illustrate a Top story using the ideas and same structure as the story, e.g. I am top boy/girl.

Sam's Pot

Focus phonics				
s	Sam	*g*	got
m	Sam Pam mop	*p*	pot pat mop
c	cat	*a*	Sam a Pam pat
t	Tom got pot pat	*o*	got pot mop

Introducing the phonics

- Read familiar rhyming poems and stories. Stop before the rhyming word and get the children to supply it.
- *Spot the Rhymes*
  Display pictures (or objects) of rhyming things (*cat, mat, bat, pot, cot, dot, mop, top, shop, map, cap, tap, dog, log, mug, rug, bug*). Ask the children to come up and find two things that rhyme, ask everyone else to put their thumbs up if they agree.
- Pick two pictures that share only the same end sound (*cat, pot, top, map, bug, dog*). Say the words, stressing the end sound and ask the children what sound they can hear at the end of these words. Ask the children to show you the letter used to make this sound using letter cards or whiteboards.
- *Robot Talk*
  Use a puppet or a robot made out of junk materials to say words in a special robotic way. Tell the children the robot says all the sounds in words separately and they have to blend the sounds together to tell you what the robot is saying. Make the robot say one of the words for the rhyming pictures (e.g. *c – a – t*), and tell the children to look at the pictures to help them.

Before reading

- Ask the children to look at the letters in the box on the back cover of their books and tell you the sound usually made by each letter in words. Can the children think of any words that begin or end with any of these letters?

- Tell the children that the words in this book use these letters so they can sound out each letter and blend them together to read the words.
- Ask the children to find and point to the first word on the first page, then look at the picture on pages 4 and 5 and find the same word written on the picture (*Tom*). Remind them that names and sentences begin with capital letters. Ask them to point to the matching lower case letter in the box on the cover and give the letter sound.

During reading

Encourage each of the children to read the whole book at his or her own pace, pointing at the words, sounding out and blending words they do not recognise. Listen in to each child reading and provide lots of praise and support if necessary.

- Praise the children if they can match one spoken word to one written word.
- Praise them for sounding out and blending sounds to read words.

Assessment

Observe the children to check that they can:
- confidently give the sound for all the focus letters, including the capital letters *T, P, S*
- successfully blend the three sounds for *got* together and recognise it as the word *got*
- recognise the repeated words (*pat* and *tap*) on pages 4 and 6.

Emphasise and model these skills for any child who needs help.

Returning to the text

Ask the children to
- Find the picture of a cap. Find a picture of something else which rhymes with *cap*. (*map, tap*) Think of other words that rhyme with cap. (*gap, lap, nap, yap, chap, clap, flap*)
- Segment *cap* into its separate sounds ready for writing. Have a go at writing *cap* on a whiteboard. Blend the sounds together again.
- *Change One Letter*
  Ask the children to change one letter of *cap* to write *map*, then *tap*, then *tag*.

- Find the word *pot* in the text. Think of other words that rhyme with *pot* (*dot, hot, got, jot, lot, not, rot*).
- Shut the book and segment *pot* into its separate sounds ready for writing. Have a go at writing *pot* on a whiteboard. Blend the sounds together again. Find it in the book to check.
- *Change One Letter*
  Ask the children to change one letter of *pot* to write *got*, then *cot*, then *cop*.

Observe the children to check that they can:
■ generate words which rhyme
■ segment *cap* and *pot* into their separate sounds, remembering the letters which represent those sounds.

Model the appropriate responses for children who need help. Follow this up with further practice using the Blending Activity, Letter Pattern Activity and Segmenting Activity for *Sam's Pot* on the *Songbirds CD-ROM*, as well as additional practice reading *Sam's Pot* using the Talking Story version.

Where next?
Further practice
Ask the children to
- Find the picture of the cat. Find a picture of something else which rhymes with *cat*. (*mat*) Think of other words that end with the sound *t*. (*bat, sat, pot, cot, not*)
- Segment *mat* into its separate sounds ready for writing. Write *mat* on a whiteboard, saying each sound in isolation as you write it. Then blend the sounds together while pointing at each sound. Find it in the book to check.

Extension
Ask the children to help write and illustrate a Rhyme Book. Develop the sentence *Tom got a pot* in a shared writing session. Finish these sentences with a rhyming word:

Pat got a ...	*(cat, mat)*
Dot got a ...	*(pot, cot)*
Mog got a ...	*(cog, log)*
Pop got a ...	*(mop, top).*

Bob Bug

Focus phonics				
r	rug rat	*s*	has sip
l	lid	*m*	mum
d	dad lid bad	*c*	cup cot
b	Bob bug big bad	*t*	fit it cot rat
f	fit	*g*	bug big mug rug hug
h	has his hug	*p*	cup sip
i	is his big fit it lid sip	*a*	has dad bad rat
u	bug mum cup rug	*o*	Bob cot

Introducing the phonics

- Make letter cards by writing the focus letters on individual pieces of card. Stress the correct letter formation as you do so and encourage the children to skywrite the letters.
- *Quick Sounds*
  Ask the children to say the sound usually made by each letter as you point to it. Vary the order.
- *Blending Sounds*
  Draw three boxes in a row, as a phoneme frame, on a whiteboard. Display the letter cards (or magnetic letters) around it. Pick three cards and place them, one in each box, to make a word (*bug, hug, rug, lid, hip, fit*). Tell the children that each of these letters makes one sound in a word. Ask the children to say the sound of each letter as you point to it then blend the letters together to read the word.

Before reading

- Ask the children to tell you the sound usually made by each letter in the box on the back cover of their books.
- Tell the children that the words in this book use these letters so they can sound out each letter and blend them together to read the words.
- Look carefully at the *b* and *d*. Ask the children to make a bed shape by putting their fists together and sticking their thumbs upwards. Point out that the left hand makes the beginning sound of *bed*, a *b* and the right hand makes the end sound, *d*.

During reading

Encourage each of the children to read the whole book at his or her own pace, pointing at the words, sounding out and blending words they do not recognise. Listen in to each child reading and provide lots of praise and support if necessary.

- Praise the children if they can match one spoken word to one written word
- Praise the children for sounding out and blending sounds to read words.

Assessment

Observe the children to check that they can:
- match one spoken word to one written word
- confidently give the sound for all the focus letters
- successfully blend the three sounds for *mum* together and recognise it as the word *mum*
- correctly sound out the *b* and *d* in *bad* on page 6, without confusion.

Emphasise and model these skills for any child who needs help.

Returning to the text

Ask the children to
- Explain what frightened Bob Bug. (A shadow in the shape of a rat.) Explain what made him feel better. (A hug.)
- Make a *b* with their left fist. Find a word in the text beginning with the sound *b*, sound out all the letters in the word and then blend them together to read the word. (*bug, big, bad*)
- Find something else in the pictures that begins with the sound *b*. (*bib, bat, bus*)

- Segment *bib* into its separate sounds ready for writing and write it on a whiteboard. Blend the sounds together again to read the word.
- Make a *d* with their right fist. Find a word in the text ending with the sound *d*, sound out all the letters in the word and then blend them together to read the word. (*dad, lid, bad*)
- Shut the book. Segment *bad* into its separate sounds ready for writing and write it on a whiteboard. Blend the sounds together again to read the word. Find it in the book to check.

Assessment

Observe the children to check that they can:
- ■ follow the meaning of the text recalling significant events
- ■ remember the sound and correct orientation of the letters *b* and *d*
- ■ segment *bib* and *bad* into their separate sounds, remembering the letters which represent those sounds.

Model the appropriate responses for children who need help. Follow this up with further practice using the Blending Activity, Letter Pattern Activity and Segmenting Activity for *Bob Bug* on the *Songbirds CD-ROM*, as well as additional practice reading *Bob Bug* using the Talking Story version.

Where next?

Further practice

- Ask the children to segment *big* into its separate sounds ready for writing. Write *big* on a whiteboard, saying each sound in isolation as you write it. Then blend the sounds together while pointing at each sound. Find it in the book to check.
- Ask the children to segment *bug* into its separate sounds and write it on a whiteboard.
- *Change One Letter*
  Ask the children to change one letter of *bug* to write *rug*, then *hug*, then *hut*, then *hum*.

Extension

Ask the children to draw characters from the story from their own families. Add speech bubbles calling out names (*Mum! Dad! Bob Bug!*) Explain that the exclamation mark shows that the characters are calling.

Dig, Dig, Dig!

Focus phonics			
r	rag	*s*	bus lots bugs
l	lot lid lots	*m*	Tim mud
d	dog dig had dug mud lid and	*t*	Tim lot tin it lots
b	bus big bugs	*g*	dig dog dug rag big bugs
f	fun	*p*	up
h	his had	*a*	had rag and
i	dig Tim his lid big tin in it	*o*	dog lot lots
u	fun dug up mud bus bugs	*n*	fun tin in and

Introducing the phonics

- *Robot Talk*
  Use a puppet or a robot made out of junk materials to say words in a special robotic way. Tell the children the robot says all the sounds in words separately and they have to blend the sounds together to tell you what the robot is saying. Make the robot say words using the focus phonics (e.g. *b – a – g, r – u – g, b – u – n*). Display objects or pictures to help the children if you have them.
- *Spot the Vowel Sound*
  Display letter cards of the focus vowel sounds, *a, i, o, u*. Tell the children that you are going to say some words that have these letters in the middle. Say a word containing one of these vowels (*cat, bib, mop, rug*). Ask the children to show you the letter used to make this sound using the letter cards, letter fans or whiteboards.
- *Blending Sounds*
  Introduce the plural *s* and practice blending sounds. Draw four boxes

in a row, as a phoneme frame, on a whiteboard. Display the focus letter cards (or magnetic letters) around it. Write the numeral *2* in front of the frame then pick three cards and place them, one in each of the first boxes (*cat, mat, mop, pot, rug, lid*). Ask the children to say the sound of each letter as you point to it, then blend the letters together to read the word. Read the whole phrase e.g. *2 cat*. Ask the children what is wrong. Ask someone to come and put the correct letter in the end sound box to make the word say e.g. *cats*. Repeat for other words, changing the numeral to *3, 4,* etc. Stress the adding of *s* at the end when there is more than one.

Before reading

- Ask the children to tell you the sound usually made by each letter in the box on the back cover of their books.
- Tell the children that most of the words in this book use these letters so they can sound out each letter and blend them together to read the words.
- Explain that it is important when blending the sounds in a word together to check to see if it sounds like a real word. Point out that in *of*, the *f* makes an unusual *v* sound.

During reading

Encourage each of the children to read the whole book at his or her own pace, pointing at the words, sounding out and blending words they do not recognise. Listen in to each child reading and provide lots of praise and support if necessary.

- Praise them if they can match one spoken word to one written word.
- Praise them for sounding out and blending sounds to read words.
- Encourage the children to read the whole book, sounding out and blending.

Assessment

Observe the children to check that they can:
- match one spoken word to one written word
- confidently give the sound for all the focus letters
- successfully blend the three sounds for *mud* together and recognise it as the word *mud*
- correctly sound out the letters in *bugs* on page 8 and blend all four together successfully.

Emphasise and model these skills for any child who needs help.

Returning to the text

Ask the children to:

- Recall what the dog dug up in order.
- Write the things dug up in order on a whiteboard. (*rag, bus, lid, tin*) (Remind the children to segment the things into separate sounds, write the sounds down then blend them together to read what they have written. Then look in the book and to check.)
- Find words in the text with *u* as the middle vowel sound. Sound out all the letters in the words and then blend them together to read the words. (*fun, dug, mud, bus*)

Assessment

Observe the children to check that they can:

- follow the meaning of the text recalling significant events in correct sequence
- segment CVC words into their separate sounds, remembering the letters which represent those sounds
- remember the letter that makes the vowel sound *u*.

Model the appropriate responses for children who need help. Follow this up with further practice using the Blending Activity, Letter Pattern Activity and Segmenting Activity for *Dig, Dig, Dig!* on the *Songbirds CD-ROM*, as well as additional practice reading *Dig, Dig, Dig!* using the Talking Story version.

Where next?

Further practice

- Ask the children to find words in the text with *i* as the middle vowel sound. (*dig, Tim, his, lid, big, tin*) Sound out all the letters in the words and then blend them together to read the words. Think of other words containing this sound. (*wig, jig, him, hid, kid, bin, din, fin*)

Extension

Ask the children to write and illustrate a number frieze. Use consonant vowel consonant words which become plural by adding *s*. (*cat, rat, bat, hat, pot, top, mop, tap, cap, rug, mug, bug, man, can, pan, fan, pin, tin, bin, dog*)

Zak and the Vet

	Focus phonics			
v	van vet	*f*	fog
w	went wag	*h*	hit him had
y	yes	*i*	sit did in hit him
z	Zak	*u*	cut
j	Jen jab	*s*	sit yes
n	not ran in Jen and van went	*m*	him
k	Zak	*c*	cut
e	red Jen went vet get yes	*t*	sit not hit went vet cut get
r	ran red	*g*	fog get wet wag
d	did and red had bad	*a*	Zak ran and van had bad jab wag
b	bad jab	*o*	not fog

Introducing the phonics

- Make letter cards by writing the focus letters on individual pieces of card. Stress the correct letter formation as you do so and encourage the children to skywrite the letters.
- *Quick Sounds*
  Ask the children to say the sound usually made by each letter as you point to it. Vary the order.
- Ask the children to tell you which letters both make the sound c (as in cat). Make a collection of words containing the c sound. Underline the letters which makes the c sound. (e.g. <u>c</u>at, <u>c</u>up, <u>c</u>an, <u>c</u>ub, <u>k</u>it, <u>k</u>id, yu<u>k</u>)

- *Segmenting Sounds*
  Draw three boxes in a row, as a phoneme frame, on a whiteboard. Display the letter cards around it. Name a word for an animal using the focus letters (e.g. *cat, dog, hen, kid, bat, yak, rat*). Ask the children to segment the word into all its sounds and then place the three cards that make those sounds, one in each box, to write the word. Ask all the children to say the sound of each letter as you point to it then blend the letters together to read the word.

Before reading

- Ask the children to tell you the sound usually made by each letter in the box on the back cover of their books.
- Tell the children that most of the words in this book use these letters so they can sound out each letter and blend them together to read the words.
- Explain that it is important when blending the sounds in a word together, to check to see if it sounds like a real word as some words are less regular. Introduce the children to the context words (see page 5, or the inside back cover of *Zak and the Vet*) by writing them on a whiteboard. Read these words and point out the letters that make the usual sound in each word (e.g. the *h* in *he*). This will help the children to remember these words.
- Look at the cover and discuss where the story is set and what a vet does. Introduce the word *jab* to describe an injection.

During reading

Encourage each of the children to read the whole book at his or her own pace, pointing at the words, sounding out and blending words they do not recognise. Listen in to each child reading and provide lots of praise and support if necessary.

- Praise them if they can match one spoken word to one written word.
- Praise them for sounding out and blending sounds to read words.

Assessment

Observe the children to check that they can:
- match one spoken word to one written word
- confidently give the sound for the focus letters
- successfully blend the three sounds for *vet* together and recognise it as the word *vet*.

Emphasise and model these skills for any child who needs help.

Returning to the text

Ask the children to

- Find words in the text beginning with the sound *v*, sound out all the letters in the words and then blend them together to read them. (*vet, van*)
- Shut the book and segment *vet* into its separate sounds ready for writing and write the word on a whiteboard. Blend the sounds together again. Find it in the book to check.
- *Change One Letter*
  Change one letter of *vet* to write *wet*, then *web*, then *wed*, then *bed*, then *bad*, then *bid* then *bud*.
- *Speed Read*
  (You will need a list of CVC words using the focus phonics for each child – *vet, ran, yes, jam, net, can, zip, bed, jog, win, hug, kit, ten, wig, pin, yak, bug* – and a timer.) Start the timer and sound out and read as many of the words as possible before the time runs out. Count the number of words correctly read as the score. Repeat several times to better the score. (Send the lists home for homework.)

Assessment

Observe the children to check that they can:
- follow the meaning of the text
- remember the letter that makes the sound *v*
- confidently use sounding out and blending to read words out of context.

Model the appropriate responses for children who need help.

Where next?

Further practice

- Ask the children to find a word in the book where the *c* sound is represented by the letter *k*. (*Zak*) Shut the book. Segment the word into its separate sounds and write it on a whiteboard, remembering the capital letter. Blend the sounds together again to read the word. Look in the book to check.

Extension

Ask the children to design and make a poster showing how to cross a road safely.

Mum Bug's Bag

Focus phonics			
w	wet	*h*	has
y	yuk	*i*	zip fit in big
z	zip	*u*	Mum Bug bun yuk
j	jam	*s*	has gets
n	can pen in fan and bun	*m*	Mum jam
k	yuk	*c*	can
e	red pen get gets wet	*t*	fit pot get gets wet
r	red	*g*	Bug bag get gets big
d	red and	*p*	zip pen pot
b	Bug bag bun big	*a*	has fan bag can and jam
f	fit fan	*o*	pot

Introducing the phonics

- Place objects (or pictures of objects) that are written with the focus letters in a bag (*pen, cat, jug, net, can, bed, kid, wig, zip, yak, peg, cup, fan*).
- *Robot Talk*
  Use a puppet to name the things in the bag in a special robotic way. Tell the children the puppet says all the sounds in words separately and they have to blend the sounds together to tell you what the puppet is saying. Ask the children to take turns to be the puppet.
- *Segmenting Sounds*
  Draw three boxes in a row, as a phoneme frame, on a whiteboard. Display the letter cards (or magnetic letters) around it. Ask the

children to pick one of the objects from the bag, segment the word into all its sounds and then place the three cards that make those sounds, one in each box, to write the word. Ask all the children to say the sound of each letter as you point to it then blend the letters together to read the word. Point out words where the c sound is written with a letter c (*cat, cup, can*) and words where the c sound is written with a letter k (*kid, yak*).

Before reading

● Ask the children to tell you the sound usually made by each letter in the box on the back cover of their books. Ask them which letters both make the sound c (as in *cat*)?
● Tell the children that most of the words in this book use these letters so they can sound out each letter and blend them together to read the words.
● Explain that it is important when blending the sounds in a word together, to check to see if it sounds like a real word as some words are less regular. Introduce the children to the context words (see page 5, or the inside back cover of *Mum Bug's Bag*) by writing them on a whiteboard. Read these words and point out the letters that make the usual sound in each word (e.g. the h in *her*). This will help the children to remember these words.

During reading

Encourage each of the children to read the whole book at his or her own pace, pointing at the words, sounding out and blending words they do not recognise. Listen in to each child reading and provide lots of praise and support if necessary.
● Praise them if they can match one spoken word to one written word.
● Praise them for sounding out and blending sounds to read words.
● Encourage the children to read the whole book, sounding out and blending.

Assessment

Observe the children to check that they can:
■ match one spoken word to one written word
■ confidently give the sound for all the focus letters
■ successfully blend the three sounds for *red* together and recognise it as the word *red*
■ read the word *yuk* on page 7 with expression.
Emphasise and model these skills for any child who needs help.

Returning to the text

Ask the children to:

- Recall what Mum had in her bag in order. (*pen, fan, bun, jam*)
- Write the things in Mum's bag on a whiteboard. (Remind the children to segment the words into separate sounds, write the sounds down then blend them together to read what they have written. Then look in the book to check.)
- *Change One Letter*
  Change one letter of *jam* to write *jab*, then *job*, then *jot* then *jet*, then *net*, then *nut*, then *but*, then *bit*.

Assessment

Observe the children to check that they can:

- follow the meaning of the text recalling events in correct sequence
- segment CVC words into their separate sounds, remembering the letters which represent those sounds.

Model the appropriate responses for children who need help. Follow this up with further practice using the Blending Activity, Letter Pattern Activity and Segmenting Activity for *Mum Bug's Bag* on the *Songbirds CD-ROM*, as well as additional practice reading *Mum Bug's Bag* using the Talking Story version.

Where next?

Further practice

- Ask the children to find a picture in this book of something that rhymes with *can* (*pan*). Segment *pan* into its separate sounds and write it on a whiteboard. Blend the sounds together again to read the word. Change one letter to make *pen*. Look in the book and check.
- Ask the children to look in the book and find a picture of something that rhymes with *bun* (*sun*). Segment *sun* into its separate sounds and write it on a whiteboard. Blend the sounds together again to read the word. Change one letter to make it say *fun*, then *fin*.

Extension

Ask the children to write and illustrate a bag story. Use the following sentence structure: *I can fit a _ _ _ in my bag.*

Oxford Reading Tree resources at this level

There is a range of material available at a similar level to these stories which can be used for consolidation or extension.

Stage 1+

Teacher support
For developing phonological awareness
- Rhyme and Analogy First Story Rhymes
- Rhyme and Analogy First Story Rhymes Tapes
- Alphabet Frieze
- Tabletop Alphabet Mats
- Alphabet Photocopy Masters
- Card Games

Further reading
- ORT First Phonics
- Snapdragons Stories
- Glowworms Poetry
- Fireflies and More Fireflies Non-Fiction
- Branch Library – Wildsmith Books Stage 1 Pack A

Electronic
- First Phonics Talking Stories and activities
- First Story Rhymes
- Click and Explore and First Talking Stories
- Clip Art
- Clip and Explore and First Talking Stories
- Floppy and Friends CD-ROM
- ORT Online www.OxfordReadingTree.com

OXFORD
UNIVERSITY PRESS

Great Clarendon Street, Oxford OX2 6DP

Oxford University Press is a department of the University of Oxford. It furthers the University's objective of excellence in research, scholarship, and education by publishing worldwide in

Oxford New York

Auckland Cape Town Dar es Salaam Hong Kong Karachi
Kuala Lumpur Madrid Melbourne Mexico City Nairobi
New Delhi Shanghai Taipei Toronto

With offices in
Argentina Austria Brazil Chile Czech Republic France Greece
Guatemala Hungary Italy Japan Poland Portugal Singapore
South Korea Switzerland Thailand Turkey Ukraine Vietnam

Oxford is a registered trade mark of Oxford University Press in the UK and in certain other countries

© Oxford University Press 2006

The moral rights of the author have been asserted

Database right Oxford University Press (maker)

First published 2006

British Library Cataloguing in Publication Data

Data available

Cover illustration by Pauline Siewert

ISBN: 978-0-19-911385-9

10 9 8 7 6 5 4

Printed in China by Imago